From Farm to Table

From **Peanuts** to **Peanut Butter**

by Kristin Thoennes Keller

Consultant:
Leslie Wagner, Executive Director
Peanut Advisory Board
Canton, Georgia

Capstone *press*

Mankato, Minnesota

First Facts is published by Capstone Press
151 Good Counsel Drive, P.O. Box 669, Mankato, Minnesota 56002
www.capstonepress.com

Library of Congress Cataloging-in-Publication Data
Thoennes Keller, Kristin.
    From peanuts to peanut butter / by Kristin Thoennes Keller.
    p. cm.—(First facts. From farm to table)
    Includes bibliographical references (p. 23) and index.
    ISBN 0-7368-2637-8 (hardcover)
    1. Peanut butter—Juvenile literature. 2. Peanuts—Juvenile literature. [1. Peanut butter.
2. Peanuts.] I. Title. II. Series.
TP438.P4T48 2005
664′.8056596—dc22   2003023374

Summary: An introduction to the basic concepts of food production, distribution, and consumption
    by tracing the production of peanut butter from peanuts to the finished product.

Editorial Credits
Roberta Schmidt, editor; Jennifer Bergstrom, designer; Kelly Garvin, photo researcher; Eric Kudalis,
    product planning editor

Photo Credits
Algood Food Co. and Lin Caufield Photographers, 12–13
Capstone Press/Gary Sundermeyer, front cover (peanut butter), 5, 19
Georgia Department of Industry, Trade & Tourism, 10, 11
Grant Heilman Photography/Arthur C. Smith III, 14, 15, 16–17
Index Stock Imagery/Inga Spence, 8–9
PhotoDisc Inc., front cover (peanuts), back cover; C Squared Studios, 1
Tuskegee University Archives, 20
Visuals Unlimited/Inga Spence, 6–7

1 2 3 4 5 6 09 08 07 06 05 04

Table of Contents

Eating Peanut Butter

Peanut butter is a popular food. People spread it on bread. Some people eat it right out of the jar. Peanut butter also can be used in **recipes**.

Peanut butter has to be made before people can eat it. Making peanut butter takes many steps.

Fun Fact!
Every year, people in the United States eat enough peanut butter to cover the floor of the Grand Canyon.

Starting with Peanuts

Peanut butter is made from peanuts. Peanuts are the seeds of peanut plants. Peanuts grow inside a shell under the ground. Peanuts also are called groundnuts and goobers.

Fun Fact!
Peanuts are not nuts. They are part of the bean family of foods.

8

Growing Peanuts

In spring, farmers plant peanut seeds. Green plants with yellow flowers grow from the seeds. Stems with flowers bend down. The stems grow into the ground. Peanuts grow at the ends of these stems.

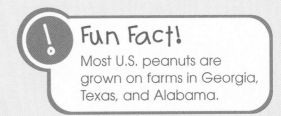

Fun Fact!
Most U.S. peanuts are grown on farms in Georgia, Texas, and Alabama.

Picking Peanuts

In fall, farmers use machines to pull up the peanut plants. Farmers let the plants dry in the field for a few days.

Farmers use **combines** to separate the peanuts from the plants. The peanuts are then dumped into wagons. Farmers sell the peanuts at buying stations.

Shelling Peanuts

Peanuts go from the buying stations to shelling plants. People and machines take the peanuts out of their shells. The peanuts are put in boxes and bags. Some peanuts are sold to stores. Other peanuts are sold to **factories** to be made into peanut butter.

Fun Fact!

In the United States, about 2 billion pounds (900 million kilograms) of peanuts are made into peanut butter each year.

Making Peanut Butter

At the factories, machines clean and roast the peanuts. Other machines **grind** the peanuts into peanut butter. Sugar and salt are added to the peanut butter.

Peanuts are oily. Peanut oil will separate from the peanut butter. **Ingredients** are added to keep the oil and peanut butter mixed together.

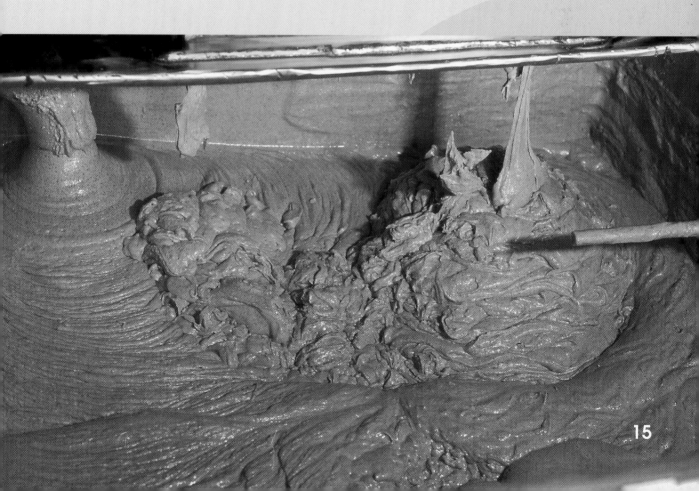

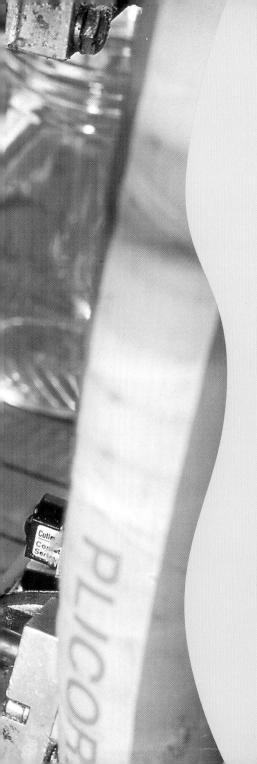

To the Store

Machines squirt the peanut butter into jars. To make crunchy peanut butter, chopped peanuts are added. Companies sell the peanut butter to stores. Trucks and trains carry the peanut butter to the stores.

Fun Fact!
A 12-ounce (340-gram) jar of peanut butter has about 520 peanuts in it.

Where to Find Peanut Butter

Grocery stores, gas stations, and many other stores sell peanut butter. Most stores sell different kinds of peanut butter. It can be creamy or crunchy. Some stores sell peanut butter mixed with jelly.

Fun Fact!
March is National Peanut Month in the United States. November is Peanut Butter Lovers Month.

Amazing but True!

George Washington Carver thought of more than 300 ways to use peanuts. He is called the Peanut Wizard. In the early 1900s, Carver experimented with peanuts and other plants. He found ways to use peanuts in foods, drinks, makeup, and medicine.

Hands On: Make Peanut Butter

You can make your own peanut butter at home. Ask an adult to help you.

What You Need

spoon
1 tablespoon (15 mL) peanut oil
1½ cups (360 mL) unsalted, roasted peanuts
large mixing bowl
food processor or blender
bread or crackers

What You Do

1. Mix the peanut oil with the nuts in the bowl.
2. Pour the mixture into the food processor or blender.
3. Chop the nuts in the food processor or blender. Blend them until the mixture is smooth and creamy.
4. Serve your peanut butter on bread or crackers. Share your peanut butter with friends.

Glossary

combine (KOM-bine)—a large farm machine that is used to gather crops

factory (FACK-tuh-ree)—a building where products are made in large numbers; factories often use machines to make products.

grind (GRINDE)—to crush something into fine pieces

ingredient (in-GREE-dee-uhnt)—an item used to make something else

recipe (RESS-i-pee)—directions for making and cooking food

Read More

Boten, Wallace. *From Farm to Store.* Compass Point Phonics Readers. Minneapolis: Compass Point Books, 2004.

McKissack, Patricia, and Fredrick McKissack. *George Washington Carver: The Peanut Scientist.* Great African Americans. Berkeley Heights, N.J.: Enslow, 2002.

Nelson, Robin. *From Peanut to Peanut Butter.* Start to Finish. Minneapolis: Lerner, 2004.

Internet Sites

FactHound offers a safe, fun way to find Internet sites related to this book. All of the sites on FactHound have been researched by our staff.

Here's how:
1. Visit *www.facthound.com*
2. Type in this special code **0736826378** for age-appropriate sites. Or enter a search word related to this book for a more general search.
3. Click on the **Fetch It** button.

FactHound will fetch the best sites for you!

Index